In memory of

Ralph B. Ellis
World War I Veteran

and

John Victor Melink
World War II Veteran

TABLE *of* CONTENTS

PREFACE

This book was a labor of love for my co-author, Monica Melink, and me. It is filled with personal experiences, stories, and fact-based research on navigating this maze called life. It also outlines step-by-step solutions that explain how one can improve, based on the lesson the reader desires.

The authors' point of view is that adversity confronts us all at certain times in life, but we believe these particular lessons can enable us to take on the real world more easily and successfully overcome the inevitable barriers.

Each chapter's layout includes four basic parts. The first section is the content regarding the chapter's *Life Lesson*, which describes why that specific lesson is important. The second is the *Coach's Corner*, which summarizes a personal story or example that illustrates the message. The third is a *Research Says* section, which identifies the research that validates the lesson. The last section is the *Coach's Playbook*, which clarifies how the readers can improve that lesson area.

For nearly 30 years, I have been a professor at both Indiana University and Butler University. For 24 of those years, I have been employed full-time at the Kelley School of Business in Bloomington, Indiana. For the last 15 years, I have coached the IU sales teams in various sales competitions held throughout the United States. Prior to becoming an educator, my business career was spent with Procter & Gamble and Xerox in various positions, including national account manager, major account sales manager, regional sales operations manager, and manager for training and development. I explain this to you because for the last 35 years, my life has been focused on influencing, developing, and coaching students and businesspeople alike to become the best they can be—both in their chosen professions and in their lives.

It surprises my students when I explain to them in the first week of the semester that "Life is not fair—better start getting used to it." The good news is that we control our destinies in the sense that each and every one of us makes decisions. Sometimes, the hard decisions don't work out. Sometimes, the easy decisions don't work out either.

However, I believe life was meant to be FUN! (There is more regarding this belief later in the book.) In the end, I mildly disagree with the Greeks during Aristotle's and Socrates' era for asking if we lived our lives with passion. Yes, passion is absolutely crucial. However, I think that true passion comes once happiness is achieved. The preferable question is: Did you live your life in happiness?

Although we try to model each of the lessons we suggest, it is unrealistic to think we won't fall down occasionally. (My family might think the words "fall down occasionally" should be translated to "fall down MORE than occasionally.") Personally, I accept the belief that an error does not become a mistake until you refuse to correct it. No one is perfect, and no one is going to be perfect. However, we can always strive to better ourselves. Even if that improvement is only a slight upgrade, at least it is positive movement in the right direction.

Unfortunately, there may be days and weeks when we slide backwards due to the adversity we face and our reaction to the hurdles in life. However, we can always climb back on that proverbial horse and live to ride for another day, always determined to move forward.

My co-author has done a good job living up to these lessons while a student in the Kelley School of Business. She played varsity soccer and maintained a very high grade point average. She also served on the executive board of the distinguished Global Sales Workshop (also known as the Global Sales Leadership Society). She is also blessed to have parents who also served as excellent role models for these lessons.

Today, Monica works for the Kraft Heinz Company as a customer category manager. She began her career in their management development program. Unlike me, a baby boomer, she is a millennial. We are different in several ways, but we are very similar in that we try to excel at each of these lessons on a daily basis. We have some bad days alongside the good, but we always try.

Occasionally, I wonder if we wouldn't be better off in life with lower standards and less stress and pressure. It'd be nice just go out enjoy life by defining success as simply whether we are happy or not. Fortunately, the primary measure of success I have used throughout my life has simply been if I was happy as a person. I believe I score 98 percent in that area. It was certainly refreshing to learn that Monica felt the same way. We hope that each of our readers, friends, family, and students will also experience a happy life, if you are not already living your dream!

We are hopeful that each reader will not need every one of the lessons, but instead have two, three, or four lessons on which to focus. You should prioritize the lesson that you believe will be most helpful to yourself. After you achieve success with a particular lesson, you should move on to the next lesson, and so on.

There is no order or priority of one lesson over another. It all depends on the person, and which lesson inspires or motivates you to act and execute it. There is no secret or underlying message to our compilation of lessons. We wish everyone could be the best they can be, but recognize there is no such thing as perfect. There will always be people better than us, but that doesn't mean that each of us can't be competitive and develop our own talents with which to navigate through the real world—and simply be happy!

MASTER ARTICULATION – DON'T RAMBLE!

"The single biggest problem in communication
is the illusion that it has taken place."
– George Bernard Shaw

· ·

How many times have you found yourself stuck in a conversation with someone who just goes on and on? Would it be fair to say that countless excessively lengthy stories, emails, and lectures end up being ignored?

Some politicians believe the quantity of words in an interview is more important than the quality of their message when they're on the air. Learn from the moments in which you are trapped in an endless whirlwind of someone else's words. Even William Shakespeare weighed in on the dangers of rambling when he wrote, "it is a tale; Told by an idiot, full of sound and fury, Signifying nothing."

What Do People Want to Hear?

In general, people are not looking for complexity. They want simplicity. They are not impressed that you can use every word from the advanced vocabulary portion of the SAT. Simply put, your credibility is not established by the number of words you get "on the air," but how succinctly you are able to deliver a message to your audience.

When you ramble during a story, you run the risk of losing the other person's attention, causing them to tune you out. Not only have you missed the opportunity to communicate your story, opinion, or ideas, but you also may alienate people from listening to you in the future.

Research Says

The University of Kent outlined the importance of "spoken" communication on its webpage, "Communication Skills: Speaking and Listening." There is an emphasis on being able to "express ideas and views clearly, confidently and concisely in speech, tailoring your content and style to the audience and promoting free-flowing communication." Without listening intently to your audience, you miss the opportunity to convey a message that resonates with the other party. If communication is one sided, it is not going anywhere but in one ear and out the other.

Included on the webpage is information from Association of Graduate Recruiters. A survey of employers offered insight into the skill sets of recent college grads. Communication skills were ranked the second most lacking quality among graduates, according to percentage of employers surveyed. Sixty-four percent of employers shared this belief. Leadership was third. What does that mean? Does the most recent generation grasp the importance of active listening, followed by precise articulation?

It is not easy to explain a complex subject in simple terms. Professors and teachers alike are challenged by the idea of simplicity. In academia, we are often expected to make a subject more complex than necessary while crafting articles for high-level research publications. Is complexity required? In academic publishing, the answer is normally yes because the research subjects tend to be of a very complex nature.

However, teachers can improve in communicating about topics more clearly by using data and visual aids. Think back to the last time you listened to a teacher lecture utilizing only his voice. Now, think of the last time you attended a lecture where a teacher communicated both verbally and through visual aids, such as PowerPoint. Which lecture engaged you more?

Another example of when the simple is not so simple: Scott Inks, a former student of mine asked me what I thought of the trust factor in sales between a seller and buyer. At first blush, I thought, "What an easy question."

However, Scott wasn't the type of person to ask questions that had simple answers. I knew he had an ulterior motive, but I decided to play along with him anyway.

"Of course, it's important," I replied. "There needs to be a trust relationship which will cause the buyer to want to work with this particular salesperson."

"So how do you know the 'trust' bond results from the seller's character and personality and isn't a result of the reputation of the seller's company? Don't some people trust companies and not necessarily the salesperson?" Scott continued. "What about the product? Perhaps the buyer really likes the product and not the salesperson? Which one of those factors is more important in establishing 'trust' than the others, or are all three equal?"

As you can see, what appeared to be a simple discussion became much more complicated. It required additional description to adequately address the issue, but how important is it to explain everything thoroughly?

In my experience, the answer lies with your audience.

Why Both Parties Matter

If the audience is engaged and continues to ask questions, this may signal that they are interested in further details. At any rate, please be sensitive to your audience and their level of interest. What seems fascinating to you may not hold their attention. Simply put, if you aren't actively listening to your audience, your message won't resonate with them.

Think about this: Are you giving your audience the opportunity to ask questions? Do you ever put the ball in *their* court to make a responsive point and drive the conversation? If you are unsure, you may have already lost them. Seems simple, yet how frequently do you find yourself on one end or the other? Those who ramble waste ample time, and people *do* notice. It is a habit that hinders our society, at work, in the classroom, and even at home.

So what do you do in cases like this one, when it takes more words to provide a satisfactory answer than time permits?

Coach's Corner

Two examples come to mind of when a question requires considerable explanation. The first is a common challenge for college students: internship and job interviews. How can students adequately convey their qualifications in only a few words?

For example, a recruiter interviewing college students and recent graduates may ask a question that targets several attributes. One such question could be, "Would you explain to me a time when you took a leadership initiative and solved a critical problem?" For a high school student, the question may simply be, "Can you tell me a little about yourself?"

One method that I use in my classes to point out the importance of being concise is a game that I call "The Articulation Game." In it, I pose a question to the students and ask them to articulate their answer to the class. It is not easy to keep answers succinct, so most students initially struggle and begin to ramble.

Some students actually enjoy playing the game. Many students are happy to observe because we assign a letter grade ranging from A to F. Who wants to receive a failing grade for their effort? After a while, most of the students get into the flow of the game and recognize that it is okay to try even if they don't earn an A or a B. It does not affect any of their documented grades. It is simply done in the spirit of developing a new and valuable skill.

I recall Albert Einstein, the creator of the theory of relativity and a Princeton physics professor, who noted, "I never teach my pupils, I only attempt to provide the conditions in which they can learn."

I feel this way regarding "The Articulation Game." It provides an opportunity for students to focus on a vital part of their social skill set. This part permits them to reveal their thoughts and opinions to the world through verbal communication.

First Impressions

A friend who is an author once explained to me, "People judge other people more by how they articulate compared to how they look today." I believe he was on to something. When students are able to express their positions clearly, crisply, and concisely, they tend to gain a reputation for having solid mastery of a topic. Some students at the college level do not always pay attention to their appearance because of the late hours they keep and the time they have budgeted (or not budgeted) in the morning to get ready. Perhaps they prioritize sleep over appearance, but their articulation skills matter the most!

Think of it this way. When you check into a hotel or you are at a lunch where the attendees are wearing "uniforms," you are unable to evaluate them by their attire. If they all seem to have their hair combed, styled, and at least appear clean, then how do you evaluate the person? Initially, you evaluate them based on how they explain or ask questions, including from tone and volume, and the actual words they speak. (Admittedly, if they don't perform, you don't care how they appear or talk.) It is not necessarily a conscious process, but it occurs at some level within each of us.

Communication in the Real World

Let's capture this concept of conciseness by looking at emails. One executive from a blue-chip consumer company tends to communicate to his people by email instead of by phone or in-person meetings. Nothing is wrong with this approach, but he tends to write two- or three-page emails. Now, there is something wrong with that because his people tune out and don't read the entire email. In the end, his communication is not effective because it does not achieve the results he wanted. He would have been better off just providing an executive summary of bullet points in a half-page correspondence. Then, he would have a better likelihood of his employees fully reading and absorbing his emails.

Another example of conciseness is noted in Sir Winston Churchill's social discourse with his antagonist Lady Astor. During a tension-filled discussion, Lady Astor allegedly told Churchill that if she was married to him, she would poison his tea. Churchill immediately responded succinctly, "Madame, if I were your husband, I would drink it."

Former U.S. President Ronald Reagan was known as a master communicator for his simplicity and clarity. While most people talked about land size in terms of acres, he spoke of land "the size of a football field," knowing that a field accurately represented one acre. It was a relatable "picture word" for Americans who needed to easily comprehend the concept.

There is no substitute for effective articulation when it comes to communicating verbally with others. Keep in mind that it is not about the quantity of airtime, but about the quality of your message.

One of my favorite quotes about a concise message is from William Strunk, Jr., a Cornell English professor. Though he was talking about writing, his message applies to speaking and talking. He stated, "Vigorous writing is concise. A sentence should contain no unnecessary words and a paragraph no unnecessary sentences for the same reason that a drawing should have no unnecessary lines and a machine should have no unnecessary parts. This requires not that the writer make all sentences short or avoid all detail and treat subjects only in outline, but that every word tell."

In the end, this is the most important question regarding articulation: "Is the message you are conveying accurate, concise, and clear—and perhaps, in rare circumstances, clever?" Abide by the three C's, and you will be surprised by how well people respond.

So how do we fix low-to-moderate articulation skills? As outlined in the solutions section, the devil is in the details. As long as you're asking the right questions and practicing a few of my techniques, you'll be well on your way to an "A" in articulation. It is not as difficult as you might imagine, but it does take time! Let's move to the *Coach's Playbook* to identify key points for improving articulation.

COACH'S PLAYBOOK

Master Articulation—Don't Ramble!

Let's discuss the questions that recruiters often ask college and high school students: "Would you explain to me a time when you took a leadership initiative and solved a critical problem?" and "Can you tell me a little about yourself?" Below are guidelines I borrowed from my journalism days that a student should consider before responding.

1. Start your answer with facts such as who, what, when, and where. These answers are brief. An example might be: "My chemistry group of eight students competed against twelve other college teams in a new pesticide competition held last spring semester in Princeton, New Jersey."

2. In the case of a high school student, it may sound like, "In my early years, my focus was on athletics and academics, but that changed in a big way when I turned sixteen. -. Let me explain." You get the idea.

Now all that's left is to address "why" a leadership hole existed and "how" you filled it.

Additional Techniques

- Speak like news broadcasters who work for major networks. These anchors are able to take 10- to 30-minute stories and condense them into 30- to 120-second segments. Observe how they use fewer words than most to communicate their messages.

- Practice and practice more. Read a newspaper article comprised of multiple paragraphs. Focus on the who, what, when, where, why, and how details of the article to condense it into one or two paragraphs.

- Use technology—from recording devices to smartphones to video cameras—to practice and grade yourself asking these questions:

  1. Was my message accurate?

  2. Was my message concise?

  3. Was my message clear?

  4. Could I have delivered my message in a more lively fashion while not making it longer? (Don't strive for entertainment at the expense of an accurate, concise, and clear message.)

TAKE A LEAP AND FAIL – DON'T BE PERFECT

"I have not failed. I've just found 10,000 ways that won't work."
– Thomas A. Edison

. . . .

This is perhaps our favorite of the 10 *Life Lessons*. Why? One reason is that the notion of failure is so easily pushed aside from what we view as acceptable. Too often, we believe it is frowned upon by society. Therefore, people become stuck in one of two worlds where:

A. perfection is the only answer
B. feeling content means no failure.

People so often forget that failure makes us human. It makes us relatable. More importantly, failure allows us to see a different side of the picture that we otherwise would not have seen.

Research Says

Failure alone is not necessarily the defining factor in ultimate success. In the *Psychology Today* article "Challenging Success-via-Failure," Carlin Flora noted that the experience of failure builds something much more deeply rooted and harder to identify—character. Being told you aren't good enough at something isn't necessarily going to make you better at it, but the experience may help you develop a sense of urgency to improve. This process can drive people to succeed.

I've always told my students what I believe to be a captivating thought: The more you can practice getting comfortable with being uncomfortable, the more opportunities will be presented to you, and the more freely you will live.

How liberating is it to know that making mistakes is essential for building success? How confining would life be if all we did is strive for perfection?

That being said, nobody wants to fail. While you and I may not intend to fail, the string of mistakes and errors become so very necessary to the journey towards success. Show me someone who does not have a string of failures assigned to his or her name, and I will show you a person who has not ascended to the top of his or her chosen profession. If you don't fail, you are not getting far enough out of your comfort zone to enable yourself to live life on *your* terms.

Using Failure to Find Success

Part of life is learning and accepting that you are not always going to get the "A" you desired nor are you always going to nail the interview for a summer internship. You will fail sometimes, which is a good thing. It is in failing that you learn how to be successful.

There is a saying I remember from my early days at Xerox: "Successful people form the habit of doing things that failures just don't do." This doesn't mean that successful people always enjoy doing those things, but they do them anyway, focusing on the long-term value of their decisions. They have learned enough from their own experiences to understand which actions work and which don't. These people know how to deal with the roadblocks when they come—and they certainly do come—because they have been through them before. If you have the tendency to strive for perfection all the time, cut yourself a break and try something completely new. It will be your steepest learning curve.

Stepping Out of Our Comfort Zones

We can settle all we want or we can reach our true potential by stepping outside of our boundaries and allowing ourselves to run into trials. Not only does it build thick skin, it also enables us to grow. If we become too content lingering in our own little world—talking to the same people, going the same places, repeating the same actions—chances are, we won't get far in life. Those who break free of their habits and learn to deal with uncertainty and failure are the ones who ultimately find the keys to success. These individuals are the ones who find true freedom through trial and error because they discover their limitless potential.

I once asked one of my former student athletes why she chose to attend Indiana University. She told me about her decision to commit to a Division I school, where she knew she would be challenged both academically and athletically. Her goal was to compete against the best rather than potentially being a star player at a Division II or III school.

She realized that if she attended a smaller college where she had less competition, she would have played every game. A scholarship would be presented. Practices would be easier. Perhaps the coaches would favor her. Off-season would be more relaxed, allowing more time to focus on school and succeed academically. However, she rejected the path of least resistance and decided to play at the highest level she could even if it meant making sacrifices in the short term and facing numerous challenges along the way.

As a freshman, she joined the team without an athletic scholarship. She was red-shirted almost immediately since her skills were not up to the level of the Big Ten. Although she worked hard and passed the fitness tests, she continuously got crushed in practice and played in zero games. Coaches had to focus on developing and supporting the players who would win games, not the practice players who could barely keep up.

While she was able to travel with the team for away games, this student explained that not being able to play in an official match was a blow to her confidence. "It was clear I wasn't up to par (talent-wise) with a lot of these players," she said, "but I never expected how hard it would be giving 110 percent in practice every day, knowing I still wouldn't see a minute on the field." She then went on to say, "I started questioning if I had chosen the wrong path."

It's indeed a challenge sticking with something when the outcome or results are nowhere in sight. To her, it was a risk worth taking. She loved the game and wanted to succeed.

A Turning Point

Although she was ultimately rejected her first year, she still hoped that she could earn playing time in subsequent seasons. She explained that the most challenging moments—although frustrating—were essential in preparing her for what it took to become better. "Any of us who didn't play in games were required to do extra workouts, compensating for any fitness lost sitting on the bench. We would wake up early in the morning before anyone else got up for regular practice, and run before the sun came up. Those were no easy feats, and it tested my mental toughness. However, it was through that adversity that made me want to make it even more."

She knew she had to get better in something to get noticed. When she focused on becoming the fittest she could be, she saw more and more results in practice. Coaches had to discipline her for messing up time after time, but she shook it off and took it as a learning experience. In her eyes, getting yelled at was better than not getting acknowledged at all. She took the pain with the punches and kept focused.

As my former student had anticipated before playing at a Division I school, she faced barriers along the way. But the beauty of the story is that she accepted these challenges for what they were, learned how to deal with her shortcomings, got over it, worked hard, kept her head up, failed some more, and worked until she could finally play at the level she dreamed of her whole life.

After her freshman year, she played in every single game for the rest of her career. She eventually became a starter and played against some of the top teams in the nation. By her senior year, she received a full scholarship.

Throughout the whole process, she continued to be tested. "There was always a fight for the starting position," she said. "I wasn't always chosen to start every game, but I continued to push myself every week to try to earn every second I could on the field. There wasn't a better feeling than getting to play the game I loved with teammates who challenged me."

By putting herself in a position to be challenged and fully recognizing that struggles and failures would be a necessary part of her dream, she was able to develop as an athlete in her sport. Academically, her goal was to graduate from a nationally ranked business school, in which she would strive to be her best. But she didn't beat herself up for not receiving straight A's.

I asked in conclusion, "Was Indiana University the right decision for you?"

"Yes," she answered. "I don't think I would have been challenged in the same way if I had taken another route. I didn't want an easy way out. I wanted an environment that would foster as much growth as possible. I knew if I surrounded myself with the best staff, the best players, and the best program at one of the best business schools, I would learn more about myself during the next four years than I had my entire life."

Setting herself up as a small fish in a big sea allowed her to climb farther and achieve more than she had ever expected. She trusted that she would succeed eventually, and even then, she accomplished more than she ever thought she could. All from taking that first leap of faith!

Perfection is Overrated

Perhaps the biggest challenge for straight-A students is that they have never really experienced failure. They've served as academic role models for other students in high school and college, but they are often unprepared when inevitable slip-ups occur. It's the C and B students who have experienced failure academically and learned to absorb the impact of such disappointments.

So often I see students and employees build up their "safety" nets to form a perfect picture of themselves. They create boundaries and will take any measures to prevent failure. In some cases, this trait stems from growing up with parents who accept nothing but perfection. These are the people who take a hard fall somewhere down the road and take twice as long to pick themselves up compared to the kid next door who knows a thing or two about how to get up right away.

In *Life Lesson Three*, we discuss the challenges of owning your actions if you fail, compared to an attitude of victimization that frees yourself from blame.

Coach's Corner

This attitude toward failure may be a significant factor in students' future success. One of our former students, who is now a billionaire and appears on the television show *Shark Tank*, acknowledges that he was not an A student because he invested more time in his social life than his studies. As a result, he accepted less-than-perfect grades on his exams. He didn't want to fail, but he knew how to cope with it. After college, he took chances in the business world, thumbed his nose at setbacks, and the rest is history. He now owns the Dallas Mavericks and several other businesses.

In a classic business tale, a CEO was asked during an interview to what he attributed his success. He replied, "One word: experience." The interviewer, apparently unsatisfied with the CEO's answer, asked a follow-up question: "But how do you get experience?" Without blinking, the CEO immediately responded, "One word: failure." The interviewer was becoming annoyed and shot back with the last question, "Why would anyone want to fail?" The CEO quickly said, "One word: experience."

Many of our students at Indiana University genuinely want to change the world and sincerely believe they can. Whether they actually will or not is an entirely different story, but they think it's a goal within their reach. So what holds them back? I would immediately respond that it is the fear of failing and falling over the cliff. Generally speaking, too many students at the university's business school shy away from projects, events, elections, or any type of participation if they believe they will not be successful.

But isn't that a normal feeling?

Of course it is. It only becomes troublesome when a person refuses to try because he or she is afraid of falling short. I attempt to show my students that it is much better to fail in the classroom than to fail in the real world. This assumes, of course, that they are learning from their mistakes and not continuing to make them repeatedly.

What Do You Have to Lose?

For 15 years, I have coached the university's sales teams at competitions held around the country. We've participated in sales contests held at Ball State University, Florida State University, the University of Wisconsin, and Kennesaw State University, to name a few. We also participate in Indiana University's National Team Selling Competition, which is sponsored by 3M Corporation and Altria.

These competitions are excellent résumé builders for students who are looking for internships while they are in school and for sales positions after they graduate. They have every motivation to want to participate. It still surprises me that there are a number of students who decline to take part because they don't have the time to invest in being good at it.

My response is always the same: "It is not about always being good at something. It is about always *trying* to be good at something." When you attempt a new skill, you have to be prepared to fail—at least in the beginning.

The more you accept imperfection, the less you will care about how others view you and the less you will beat yourself into the ground. You'll give it your best shot without worrying about how you measure up to others. As I mentioned earlier, gaining true freedom means getting used to being uncomfortable. You free a whole new side of yourself as you become more and more exposed to discomfort. Let go of other people's opinions and your own self-judgment, and the world will seem much different.

Research Says

Organizational behavior professor Jerker Denrell explained just how crucial failure is for those who eventually come out as winners. In Marina Krakovsky's *Stanford Business Magazine* article "What We're Missing When We Study Success," she summarized a study by Denrell that argued "studying successes without also looking at failures tends to create a misleading—if not entirely wrong—picture of what it takes to succeed." Through a comparison of successful businesses and organizations, he proposes that the only common denominators among these powerhouses are the failures that their executives have encountered over the course of their careers.

So why is it that people are always focusing on the glorious outcome and not the journey full of defeat? Karakovsky noted that Denrell also said that people become blindsided when only focusing on success. Leaders at failing organizations take many of the same steps as those that are successful. The difference is that such leaders struggle to learn, make changes, and pick themselves up.

Certainly, each of us has learned from our own mistakes. I am not talking about students, either in high school or college, who are not motivated to learn because they haven't been given a personal or educational environment that is conducive to learning. It's more difficult for these students to learn because they need to show resourcefulness, motivate themselves to be disciplined, and open themselves up to being the best they can be. Easy to say but not so easy to do.

No, I'm talking about students who wish to improve themselves but are too concerned with taking a leap and failing. A successful life is not always dependent on winning—it's about learning and overcoming boundaries. Is there a successful athlete who has not failed miserably in a sport before achieving greatness? Of course not! No one on this planet—perhaps with the exception of people who have been handed opportunities without earning them—become successful without failure.

Taking Chances

The former student athlete I referred to earlier in the lesson had participated in the sport since she was four. According to her, the greatest learning experience she had in her 18 years as an athlete was the sheer number of losses her team experienced until they worked and improved enough to qualify for the NCAA tournament. Her team played its last game against the reigning national champions in the round of 32 her senior year.

Failure was injected into her psyche at a young age as being acceptable. Her eventual victories justified her previous lack of success. She was fearless when it came to sales competitions, even if she didn't perform as well as she'd hoped. This characteristic brought her to my attention. She smiles when she fails because she keeps life in perspective and recognizes that the focus is not always on her.

As you will read in the solutions section that follows, success is all about mindset. By recognizing that you will fail sometimes but by still putting yourself out there and trying anyway, you are setting yourself up for eventual victories, much like my former student.

It's like eighteenth century Irish philosopher and orator Edmund Burke said, "Nobody made a greater mistake than he who does nothing because he could only do a little." Or, as my co-author Monica Melink said, "Failure is your friend when you know how to leverage it; it can be the push of motivation to improve, and the only way to learn how to succeed."

Let's move to the *Coach's Playbook* to identify key points for improving this particular lesson regarding failure.

COACH'S PLAYBOOK

Take a Leap and Fail—Don't Be Perfect

1. Recognize the truth of the proverb "a good plan today is better than a perfect plan tomorrow."

2. Further acknowledge that no one achieves excellence without failing because this is a valuable tool in gaining experience.

3. If you want something badly enough, you can achieve many things—not all things, just many things. However, you may need to pay a higher price through practice and failure than someone else for whom that skill comes more naturally.

4. Seek out a mentor who can give you reassurance through tough times. It's amazing how certain people can put things into perspective and convince you that everything will be okay!

5. Believe that you only fail when you give up! Persistence and tenacity can offset a string of failures.

OWN YOUR ACTIONS – YOU ARE NOT A VICTIM

"Parents can only give good advice or put them on the right paths, but the final forming of a person's character lies in their own hands."
—Anne Frank

. . . .

Our society has gradually evolved from people having a sense of personal ownership for behaviors and their consequences to placing themselves in victimhood.

While this attitude permeates our education system, it doesn't stop there.

Unfortunately, this social environment provides built-in excuses and reasons why students are not successful in school and in their careers. When you give up ownership of your performance and decisions, you've taken the most important step toward a frustrating and unproductive life. Accept responsibility for yourself because you are the only person who can shape your destiny. No one has control over your fate but you!

Handling Adversity

I understand people have different circumstances. Certain upbringings, family dynamics, or financial situations—there will always be people with more or less disadvantages. While nobody can change the hand they were dealt, the message is more about acknowledging the state you are in and dealing with it. Yes, two different people may have to work more or less than the other to achieve the same feat.

The main question I have for you is: Do you work with or around certain circumstances without feeling sorry for yourself? Or are you letting those circumstances define you and hold you back from success?

In the end, you are the only one who has responsibility for your actions.

After all, the most admirable people in the world are those who find a way to succeed *regardless* of their situation. That is, those who do more *despite* having fewer resources than others are far more impressive than that focus on self-pity!

Carving Your Own Path

Nobody can determine your destiny but you. Don't leave it up to your parents to build your reputation or determine your standing. Regardless of status, it always falls back on the individual to make his or her own name.

During a recent National Football League Hall of Fame induction ceremony, Jerome Bettis, running back for the Pittsburgh Steelers, addressed his son and said, "I don't have much to give you, but I have a good name. Please don't ruin it." What a terrific gift he gave his child. Our reputations are valuable because when we tarnish or ruin them, they are difficult to restore. So avoid that struggle in the first place and develop a reputation as someone who does what is right.

Peyton Manning is another exceptional example of an athlete who accepts responsibility for his team's losses and praises his teammates when the team is victorious. He has figured out ownership of actions on his own.

Who Is to Blame?

The common denominator among all of us is our free will and the ability to use it to make decisions that affect our lives. Admittedly, some decisions are easier to make when we have unlimited money at our disposal, but often we have to do without such funding. We don't like to admit that life isn't fair. However, reality dictates that some people face much bigger challenges than others while clawing their way to the top of the ladder in their chosen field.

Perhaps one party lacked the means to attend college, limiting themselves during the course of their careers. Perhaps they didn't have the grades. So who or what was responsible for their grades? The parents? The teachers? The location of the school? Despite the other influential factors, the students themselves are ultimately in control of their academic performance. At some point, all of us need to recognize the short- and long-term consequences of our actions.

Research Says

Why do we make excuses for ourselves? Timothy Pychyl, an associate professor of psychology at Carleton University in Ottawa, Canada, wrote a *Psychology Today* blog entry. In "Hierarchy of Excuses: The Pathetic Path of Least Resistance," he addressed the strategies we use to reduce emotional dissonance and why people go about them.

Pychyl brings up interesting, but logical reasons behind our reasoning for putting blame on everyone or everything else besides ourselves. In a sense, it's a defense mechanism to avoid facing the problems we've created for ourselves. "We don't like dissonance and emotional distress," explained Pychyl.

Pychyl argued that there is an evident "preference structure" that participants use in order to lessen their dissonance. He stated that the most preferred to least are:

- *Rationalize away the behavior* (e.g., It doesn't matter what I do, it's just a drop in the bucket"),

- *Deny responsibility for our behavior* (e.g., It's not my role to do this"),

- *Distract ourselves from the dissonance itself, or the choice we made* (e.g., "I've got other things to think about right now), and, finally (only under the highest levels of distress/dissonance),

- *Change our behavior* (e.g., "I will take the time right now to address this issue").

Pychyl concluded that the "final strategy of behavioral change... is the 'best,' because it means our lives match our beliefs. We make actions to realign ourselves with our values and beliefs. In doing this, we choose to be the people we want to be." When we choose the other strategies, we become excuse makers, constantly lying to ourselves instead of facing the problem up front.

A business colleague of mine often remarked, "I don't always make the right decision, but I make the decision right." No one consistently makes perfect decisions, but we may still have the opportunity to revisit our choice and make a different one. For example, a high school senior decides not to attend college because he doesn't enjoy school. He simply may not be sufficiently disciplined at the age of 18 to put his nose to the proverbial grindstone and study.

It doesn't mean that at the age of 25, he cannot make a different choice. We have a group of students at our university that are labeled nontraditional students. These learners are often 15, 25, or even 35 years older than most college students. These nontraditional students decided that they wanted to earn their degree sometimes to better their career opportunities, but also because of a personal desire and to achieve a goal they set for themselves years earlier.

Reactive vs. Proactive

In the course of my career, I've encountered a number of people who placed themselves in the hands of others, assuming, or perhaps hoping, that they would be lead down a successful path. In the *Harvard Business Review* blog entry "Take Ownership of Your Actions by Taking Responsibility," John Coleman explained that "One of the most common momentum killers I've seen in my professional life is our propensity to wait for someone else to act, take initiative, assume blame, or take charge. But very often, no help comes."

The biggest error someone entering the workforce can make is to assume that another person controls his or her future. You are the only one who can—and will—truly look out for yourself. Regardless of where you started off, the only person in charge of the course of your life is you.

Could we say the same about minorities throughout history who fought for the rights to equal education and employment? Clearly, the discrimination they faced was initially out of their control, but they took matters into their own hands and held themselves accountable for *changing* what the world offered them. Nothing has ever been accomplished by people who sat back and hoped for change.

Are You Entitled?

What about parents who train their children to become reliant on everyone but themselves? According to Coleman, it is especially critical for millennials to overcome this mentality early on in their careers:

Millennials are history's most educated generation and often come from smaller families where helicopter parents watched over them carefully. Many managers perceive them as needing guidance, structure, and constant feedback. And in a world of political and financial bailouts, they (and other generations) may begin to see personal, professional, and social problems as issues for others to solve.

We all make decisions on a daily basis—some good, and some bad. Nevertheless, each of us needs to assume full responsibility for them. If the results are less than optimal, what part of the outcome is each of us willing to accept as our fault and not someone else's?

Empower Yourself

I've always appreciated the sentiment that you only fail when you give up. It's discouraging when you watch yourself repeatedly fail. However, as long as you keep chipping away and pushing yourself to succeed, you can maintain a high level of self-esteem and self-worth. In the end, you answer to yourself. If you assign blame elsewhere, you're giving up the one control factor in your life. It's easier in the long run to accept ownership and recognize that you are not a victim. After a certain age, no one is responsible for your decisions but you—not your parents, not your teachers, not your friends, not your family.

You are always deciding.

Coach's Corner

Whatever you want to do in your life, you probably have a semblance of a chance of making it happen. Again, some students have better odds than others, but all of us have a chance within reason.

Growing up, it was clear I wouldn't be a candidate for, say, MIT's mathematical program. I don't possess an innate knowledge or understanding of subjects like calculus. Once I accepted that, I could figure out what I might be good at. I wanted to be a high school coach at one time, but it didn't pan out, so I tried to figure out another way that I could "coach." Along came the Xerox Corporation. After a few years, I found a home in their training organization. I was simply "coaching" business people instead of high school students. Today, I "coach" college attendees on setting career goals and improving their consulting, marketing, and life skills.

There are many ways to figure out where you belong. It's terrific if someone can guide you there, but remember that you have the power to figure it out on your own. You just have to be patient, continue experimenting, and recognize that you will get there someday. The time it takes will be in direct proportion to the amount of time you invest and the passion with which you pursue it. Many people are willing to express their opinions. Take advantage of that and ask them questions.

I've observed over my last 30 years teaching at Butler University and Indiana University that the top students accept total responsibility for their grades and GPA. It's extremely gratifying when a typically superior student apologizes for a C- they earned on their exam.

The students who acknowledge their own setbacks and look for ways to learn from them are the most likely to achieve success in their lives. These students are motivated to take ownership of their results. They will transition into their careers believing that their fate lies in their own hands!

This quality extends far beyond the classroom. We can take the first steps toward making better decisions by increasing our awareness of our actions and identifying errors that we to which we may be prone. (I discuss the most common under the solutions section that follows.) If we can admit to our faults and take charge of finding answers to our own problems instead of looking for a scapegoat, we will ultimately grow more in times of trial.

Let's move to the *Coach's Playbook* to identify key points for improving this particular lesson of ownership versus victimization.

COACH'S PLAYBOOK

Own Your Actions—You Are Not a Victim

1. Recognize the fundamental truth that you are the only person responsible for your success and happiness. It's an easy first step to identify, but a difficult one to take. It means that you no longer accept reasons or excuses for your own mistakes or failure. This is a scary reality because it leaves us without a safety net, but it can make us much stronger people.

2. List the reasons why your goals, targets, objectives, projects, or career aspirations will NOT happen. Once your list is complete—you can ask other people for suggestions as well—figure out how you can eliminate each of them.

Say, for example, that you don't believe you can scrape together the money to follow your dream of opening a bookstore. You need $250,000, and your bank account is at an anemic $77.77. You realistically conclude that this is quite a mountain to climb. How do you find $250,000 if you don't have the credit power to borrow it and don't plan on stealing it?

3. Describe ways to make it happen. Perhaps you decide to save $25,000 each year for 10 years. Naturally, you don't want to wait, but working for 10 years towards your goal is a better option than NEVER achieving it. However, if you want your dream to happen immediately and refuse to make sacrifices over the next 10 years, my question is, "how important is this dream to you?"

   There is nothing wrong with allowing your goal to evolve into an entirely different one, such as buying and selling books over the Internet. You may realize that mom- and-pop bookstores are struggling today against the surge of mass-market booksellers and online retailers, so you choose a different path that still satisfies your passion for books. Wherever you end up, you know that your path is a result of conscious choices you made.

4. Adopt the viewpoint that there is a solution to every problem and it's just a matter of finding it. This is one of my primary beliefs regarding success. It requires the attitude that believes impossible is ONLY an opinion.

Life Lesson Four

BE EARLY TO THE GAME – IT'LL START WITHOUT YOU

"Arriving late was a way of saying that your own time was more valuable than the time of the person who waited for you."
—Karen Joy Fowler

. . . .

Although most people recognize the importance of being on time, some cannot actually live by it every single day. Some students have mastered this simple concept, but there are a handful that struggle greatly in being on time. Where does one draw the line to say he or she is accountable for being on time?

Why Are You Really Late?

People generally recognize that it's inconsiderate to keep others waiting and to be late to appointments. Yet some people are continuously always late. As a professor, the most fascinating part of tardiness is that many students don't realize that a few of their peers are actually punctual nearly all the time.

Here are some of the common reasons I hear from students about why they are late to my class.

1. The parking was horrendous.
2. The traffic was awful.
3. The weather was unbelievable.
4. My alarm did not go off.
5. My dog or cat ran off.
6. The meeting ran over.
7. I received a last minute phone call from my parents.

Research Says

There is no one to blame but yourself for being late. Dr. Phil McGraw, the notable TV psychologist, claimed that tardiness is a form of arrogance. "Ask yourself why you are late and/or why you put things off. What is your payoff for the behavior? You wouldn't continue unless you were getting some reward for it. Be encouraged that this behavior can change overnight," he wrote on his website.

Laura Schocker explained that "psychological components can contribute to chronic lateness," in the Huffington Post article, "This is Why You're Late All the Time (And what to do about it)," Schocker refers to a study by Diana DeLonzor at San Francisco State University. The study linked chronic tardiness to certain personality characteristics, including "anxiety, low self-control and a tendency toward thrill-seeking."

In reality there *isn't* a payoff for tardiness which is why it's a behavior that can be changed if the perpetrator is willing to focus on improvement. Those who do not change their behaviors will continue to be late to the game. Unfortunately, it becomes a lifestyle if left unaddressed.

Given these circumstances, it is always possible to improve. Refer to our chapter, "Maximize Your Time – Or You Will Never Find It." Once you prioritize your time, what excuse is there to be late? Once you gain control of your life, you'll know what you can fit in and how to make it work.

Timeliness as a Form of Respect

Over the years, I believe I have heard nearly all the excuses students give for being late to class. Regardless of the reason, I suggest students email or text me if they are going to be late or miss class. To students' credit, they run on time within a few weeks. One motivational incentive I use helps reduce class tardiness. Whenever a student is late, the entire class breaks out in applause.

It is disrespectful to keep another person waiting for you. However, there are times when lateness is unavoidable. For example, one may have a flat tire or auto accident. But, at the very least, let the other party know you will be late as soon as possible.

At this point, you may be thinking that being on time isn't a particularly new concept and that it's unnecessary to place so much focus upon timeliness. After all, there are good reasons for being late, so what's the big deal?

Simply, all tardiness can be avoided.

Dr. Phil is more blunt on his website. He claimed, "If you are always late, yet you tell yourself and others that you try to be on time, get real. You can't always be late unless you work at it. You would be on time just by accident occasionally!"

He suggested that people attempt to quit controlling the situation, stating, "When everything is about you because everyone has to wait on you, you are unfairly controlling the situation while assuming that others should and will wait on you. It's an arrogant behavior."

The primary reason we emphasize punctuality in my classes is because it is perceived as a self-oriented behavior. It is important for some students to recognize that the world is also about other people and the importance of other people's time too.

Coach's Corner

This is where timely responses and expectation levels fit. For example, Dr. Charlie Ragland, the executive director of the Center for Global Sales Leadership at Indiana University's Kelley School of Business, commented to me recently regarding why it took a particular student so long to respond to his emails. I asked Charlie what he felt was a reasonable for an email response time. He said, "Less than 24 hours." He continued to say that one student leader had taken nearly a day and half to respond to him. It seemed to be a trend, if not a pattern, for this particular student whom we both knew.

So is there response time etiquette? I don't know if there is any universally accepted timeframe for response, but this is what I suggest to my students. Today, nearly every student has a smartphone which assists him or her with adhering to these parameters.

- Text message response . . . . 2-4 hours
- Email response. . . . . 4-8 hours
- Telephone message response . . . . .Sundown!

You may be wondering about "Sundown." What does Sundown mean? It means that you return telephone calls by sundown of the day you receive them—or earlier. You may respond, "But Professor Canada, some businesspeople and students may not be available until later if at all during the evening, such as a business that closes at 6:00 p.m." Your point is well taken. However, returning phone calls before sundown does not mean you necessarily speak with the person for it to qualify as a returned call.

Are there certain situations that are exceptions to these time-frames? They include email blasts and telephone messages that are left on smartphones and landlines. Of course, we can't always be perfect. However, it's best to adopt these benchmarks.

My response rules do not apply to everyone. For instance, you wouldn't be expected to return telemarketer phone calls unless their service or product fills an immediate need for you or you are a customer. Another exception might be if the communication is of a social nature. Then you can be more lenient with your response time, particularly if the other person indicates you do not have to return their call or there is no hurry to return it.

Is there a single criterion to use when it comes to my response time rules? Yes, if the text, email, or voice message requests you to provide information such as setting up a meeting time, deciding if you want to go to dinner that evening, or meeting for coffee in the student union. In these cases, you should provide a response that follows my guidelines. However, text would be the preferred method of communication here, particularly among students.

But what about spur of the moment invitations? By all means, give it a shot but do not be disappointed if the person does not respond within the allotted time parameters suggested.

Aside from spontaneous invitations, remember the following. When you consistently show up late to appointments, meetings, and classes, or take over a day to respond to someone via email, text, or phone. you are conveying to others that their time isn't as valuable as your's. This arrogant thought isn't valued by anyone.

Luckily, chronic tardiness is a behavior that can be changed overnight if you're willing to take a few key concepts to heart (outlined in the following section).If you take responsibility for your behavior and the necessary steps to improve, the time when you took days to respond to emails or arrived five minutes late to class will be a distant memory.

Let's move to the *Coach's Playbook* to identify key points for improving this particular lesson of punctuality.

COACH'S PLAYBOOK

Be Early to the Game—It'll Start without You

1. Return messages as they come rather than setting aside a particular time each day to do so. Return messages during your "dead times" throughout the day. These times might be between classes, during lunch breaks, when you are resting, when a meeting is cancelled, when a meeting is running late, and so on.

2. Leave messages on people's voicemail informing them that you returned their call.

3. Be sensitive to returning messages when you are on dates, during meetings, at important events, and at the movie theater once the previews have started. And certainly not at a formal dinner party.

4. Vince Lombardi, the legendary coach of the Green Bay Packers, told his players that if he called an 8:00 a.m. meeting, they should all be in their seats by 7:45 a.m. Being 15 minutes early to each appointment and meeting became known as functioning on Lombardi Time.

   a. Sounds easy, right? The challenge with Lombardi Time is that students recognize they have 15-minute buffers. Therefore, they recognize they have an extra 15 minutes so it is okay if they do something else during that time. In effect, they cancel the significance of being 15 minutes early.

   b. One semester, I kept a log and nearly 85 percent of the time when I asked the tardy students if they functioned on Lombardi Time, their reply was often a sheepish no.

5. If you want to teach others to be punctual when meeting you, you must be timely yourself or the other party will feel no pressure to do the same.

6. However, what should you do when the person you are meeting runs behind, creating a domino effect for you and your later commitments? Three options exist.

   1. You simply run late to your next class or appointment.
   2. You reschedule the meeting with the person who is late.
   3. You notify your next appointment and ask if would they still be available to meet or if they would they like to reschedule?

Life Lesson Five

EARN TRUST –
ONCE IT'S BROKEN, IT'S HARD TO FIX!

*"If you don't have trust inside your company, then
you can't transfer it to your customers."*
—Roger Staubach

. . . .

Larry Thomas, my business partner in my sales research firm The Dartmouth Group, Ltd., addressed trust best when he told my class: "Once you break the bond of trust, it is difficult to regain it. Don't break it! Be ethical. Be moral. Be honest."

Research Says

UK researchers Chris Halliburton and Adina Poenaru elaborated upon this idea in a 2010 survey they conducted for Pitney Bowes at ESCP Europe Business School. They talked to 2,000 customers in the UK and the USA in banking, insurance, and mobile phone industries, and conducted interviews with senior marketing executives. Based on this data, they concluded that marketers unanimously emphasize the importance of customer trust. Thomas believes that trust is the most important characteristic that a person can offer another, an idea supported by these researchers.

Admittedly, several factors contribute to the building of trust. Three factors that resonate with us most are:

- **DWYSYWD** and honor commitments
- **Display urgency** by responding quickly
- **Laugh at yourself**, display humor

DWYSYWD

DWYSYWD is an acronym that stands for "do what you say you will do." The vast majority have not heard of this acronym. It is your "word bond" that you are going to do for another person what you said you were going to do. It means being dependable and reliable in your commitments.

Halliburton and Poenaru's research revealed that providing "customer care" or a "sense of being looked after" was based on companies "Doing what they say they are going to do."

However, some people's commitments are conditional rather than firm because they aren't following through on their word.

Why is that? It is a challenge for us to prioritize our commitments when we live in a world where we constantly are bombarded with emails, texts, infomercials, political messages, direct mail, junk mail, and invitations. It's particularly difficult when we believe a commitment we have made earlier may need to be recanted because a better offer came along.

Though there are legitimate reasons canceling or rescheduling an obligation, we are focusing on people who seem to have a higher than normal rate of changing their commitments. These people become lack dependability, sometimes simply because they are disorganized in their time and life, and cannot juggle multiple obligations.

Certainly, we have to change our minds occasionally because the consequences of our actions can be severe and cause unhappiness. However, the aftermath of breaking commitments can be long lasting, especially if people are choosing not to follow through for any particular reason. However, this can be a dangerous habit as the more frequently you back out of commitments, the greater you stand in contrast with **DWYSYWD**. Such actions weaken any trust relationships you may have established.

That being said, there still are those people who still believe in the concept of "my word is my bond." They don't need multiple page documents drafted by an attorney. They believe if they give their word, their word should be sufficient. They don't want legal advice. They want honesty. Unfortunately, not all people are willing to ensure their word is their bond or commitment. This is why so many standard legal documents, such as mortgage contracts, have grown in length over the decades. People look for loopholes that will permit them to have a more favorable outcome than what was intended.

We are not discussing these types of situations, however. In this lesson, we're focusing more on day-to-day and week-to-week commitments in business, politics, and social worlds that deserve honoring. It may be something as simple as saying, "Yes, let's go to lunch tomorrow," to a friend, only for your boss to saddle you with another two hours of work when your lunch hour arrives. Last minute changes such as these are unavoidable, but it doesn't hurt to attempt to negotiate a compromise to a deadline in order for you to keep a commitment.

However, it should be noted that in our collective experience, it seems that the people who procrastinate more frequently are more likely to break their commitments. Our point with the **DWYSYD** lesson is that there are many, many reasons for breaking commitments—some valid, some invalid, and some suspect.

In the end, some people have more last minute changes than others. What matters is how you deal with these last minute changes. We have always believed that a single instance is a data point, two instances a trend, and three instances a pattern. The pattern of breaking commitments is the most harmful in business and social relationships.

Display Urgency

The second factor in maintaining or developing trust is displaying a sense of urgency. For example, a deadline is given of April 4 at noon. Many people wait until the morning of April 4 to submit their documents or finish their tasks. This is acceptable because the deadline is met.

However, some people will treat deadlines as the end. They decide that their project is due at the beginning, not the end. These people tend to standout as more trustworthy because they tend to procrastinate less. It doesn't mean that if you wait until the last minute, but meet the deadline, that you are untrustworthy. But you tend to stand out when you meet your deadline earlier.

Halliburton and Poenaru described comments of improving communication from their interviews as "Keep me up to date on changes that save me money" or "Keep me informed of better interest rates." The quicker that companies—and people—communicate important matters, the faster the trust bond grows and the stronger it becomes. In the book *The Godfather* by Mario Puzo, one line stood out: "Mr. Corleone is a man who insists on hearing bad news at once." Just because news is not good, does not mean it should be delayed. We believe people associate bad news quickly with establishing and maintaining trust because people feel they can depend on you to be straightforward and candid in your communications. Thus, people who are candid tend to be trusted.

Coach's Corner

A few years ago, a student asked for a letter of recommendation for overseas studies. I agreed to write it, but explained it would be two weeks. The student said it needed to be finished in three days since that was the deadline. I explained that it might be difficult for me to meet that deadline. I also was interested in why the student waited so long to ask. He responded that he decided to participate only four days before the deadline because perceived monetary constraints that had been solved for him.

It was then up to me to decide if I could manage my own time and my own commitments in order to fulfill this student's request. I decided to put in the time and write the recommendation. It wasn't lost on me that if I had failed to meet his deadline, he would have been less likely to trust me in the future.

I didn't want to break the trust bond, so I created a sense of urgency that pushed me to finish his request within 24 hours. I immediately notified him when it had been completed and submitted.

Another story that highlights a sense of urgency as it relates to trust comes from the national sales manager at Cook Medical, Chip Helm. Chip is a dentist by education but changed professions and decided to pursue a career in sales. Over the years, he has returned my texts within an hour or two. It feels as if this sense of urgency is instilled in his DNA.

Chip told my classes that if there were a party that began at 7:00 p.m., he and his wife would arrive in the driveway of the hosts at 6:50 p.m., 10 minutes early. At 6:59, he and his wife would exit their car, walk up to their host's door, and knock at 7:00. There is no doubt in my mind that Chip links urgency with trust and that he does what he says he will do.

Executing **DWYSYWD** and ensuring that you **Display Urgency** are important factors when developing trust over a long period of time. Over the short term, building trust simply requires being honest, candid, and straight-forward, and disclosing your true feelings rather than manufacturing or putting a "spin" on your messages and comments.

After all, just think of the negative perception that politicians create for themselves when they put a "spin" on their responses and refuse to answer questions directly. This may be the primary reason that the "trust factor" takes a beating with so many politicians.

Laugh at Yourself

Finally, our third factor is to **Laugh at Yourself** and display humor. Often, we tend to take ourselves too seriously. One of our lessons focuses on the ability to laugh at oneself, which is why we won't discuss this element in much depth. Instead, we encourage the reader to refer back to that particular lesson. All in all, being humorous is preferable to being defensive.

Recently, a close friend of mine, Nick, had a particularly rough day. According to him, everything he touched turned to a "lump of coal". On this day, he was ALWAYS the last person who did NOT make the traffic light, ALWAYS chose the longest line at the bank and the grocery store, and could NOT get their remote opener on his garage door to work. Additionally, Nick was the person who arrived at the gas station to discover ALL the gas pumps were in use and received the WRONG order from the fast-food drive thru AFTER he had driven away.

No, it was not a good day for my friend. Yet his response to it was priceless and not negative in the least: "Perhaps these lumps of coal today will turn into diamonds tomorrow." After saying this, Nick went on his way, knowing, in all probability that he might find yet another lump of coal before the day was over. Still, he did so with a resigned smile on his face!

You couldn't help but like Nick because he was so honest in his feelings and communication. When you add his sense of humor and ability to laugh at himself into the mix, you found yourself trusting and liking him even more.

Executing the Factors of Trust

We make choices in life. Sometimes these are hard choices. It is easier said than done to laugh at adversity when it hits. However, laughing is preferable to crying, especially when your setbacks and "lumps of coal" are usually minor in the overall scheme of things.

If you can **Laugh at Yourself,** people will trust you more, but you need more than a sense of humor to establish a long-lasting relationship based on trust. You also need to execute **DWYSYWD** and **Display Urgency** on a daily basis. By combining these three ideals, we can meet commitments more frequently. However, putting these behaviors into action is easier said than done.

The next section provides a few ideas that should help with any issues you may have. Let's move to the *Coach's Playbook* to identify key points for improving this particular lesson of trust.

COACH'S PLAYBOOK

Earn Trust—Once It's Broken, It's Hard to Fix!

1. Ask yourself if this commitment is really something you want to make, assuming you have a choice. If you have no choice, accept it and inquire if you can take longer to think about it.

2. If you must cancel your commitment, try exploring alternative solutions to maintain the spirit of your commitment. For example, you could say, "I need to change my commitment, but let's reschedule to a time that is convenient for you. I will make every effort to adjust my schedule accordingly. I'm sorry."

3. It is very important to share news about changes to your ability to meet a commitment quickly. Don't delay. Develop a sense of urgency! If you anticipate that you might have to modify the parameters of a commitment, set that expectation level early, perhaps even at the time you make plans. People don't like last minute changes, especially when the other party had plenty of time to notify a person of the modification.

4. If you don't want to complete a commitment, consider the possible ramifications on the other party if you cancel. Ask the other person how important the commitment is to them. Sometimes, it is better to keep your commitment when something is important to the other party. However, this comes with a BUT. Do it with a happy heart. Do not complain because the other person may become frustrated and disappointed like you are. There is no winner in such situations.

Don't procrastinate. Yes, all of us do from time to time, but the cost of procrastination emerges later. Procrastination might cause someone to run out of time. For example, when an employer asks someone to take on a last minute project, there could no time left for that task and the person's commitment to you. A domino effect occurs when procrastination hits. Unfortunately, the dominos keep falling and falling. Procrastination has many unforeseen ramifications. Thus, the best tactic does it as rarely as possible.

5. Consider humor, particularly laughing at yourself, to build trust. But you must be authentic and genuine, not phony!

THINK FOR YOURSELF – DON'T JUST FOLLOW

"A genuine leader is not a searcher for consensus, but a molder of consensus."
—Martin Luther King, Jr.

....

Today, it is tempting to be influenced by majority thinking, particularly because students use so much social media. Sometimes the majority is correct, and sometimes the majority is wrong.

Sometimes we elect the best candidate to be the president of the United States, and sometimes we don't. Statistically speaking, it is reasonable to conclude that among the 42 presidents we have elected, from George Washington to Barack Obama, that some of the candidates who lost may have done a better job.

As Sir Winston Churchill stated, "Democracy is the worst form of government, except for all the others." Since the majority is not always correct in a democratic society, it is prudent to begin to learn to think for yourself rather than following the herd.

Who Are You Following, and Why?

Admittedly, some groups are more desirable to join than others. It's probably not a good idea to join a group known for violent behavior, gangs around school, and the bullies among your peers. You are definitely not thinking for yourself when you join such groups.

Even when you are on committees, teams, or in a class, you should form your own ideas and not just rely on the opinions of others, including your parents. At what point can you differentiate from following the beliefs of others versus developing your own viewpoints and living by your core values?

Owning Your Decisions and Actions

A defining point in our lives is the moment when we are confident enough to know what we stand for and take action to support our position. A leader cannot emerge when he or she is submissive to the influence of others. There's a silver lining in being able to identify who we are and having the courage to stand by our beliefs without concern for anyone else's opinion.

Research Says

Fred Luthans, Steve Norman, and Larry Hughes offer an interesting argument in their book, *Authentic Leadership: A New Approach for a New Time*. The authors explain the need for cognitive leaders who are not afraid to expose themselves. They touch on the importance of what they call authentic leadership development (ALD). The authors call ALD the turnaround point in one's life where he or she responds with conscious ownership instead of submissive behavior.

The authors cite studies published in journals by Bruce J. Avolio and Fred Luthans in defining the progression to authentic leadership. They describe ALD as "a process that draws upon leaders' life course ... to produce greater self-awareness and self-regulated positive behaviors, which in turn foster continuous, positive self-development resulting in veritable, sustained performance..."

> A helpful starting point for developing authentic leadership is to think for yourself and not embrace the conventional views of popularity.

As I explain to my students, there is a fine line between thinking creatively and thinking strangely. I encourage creativity in thought, particularly when it comes to succumbing to "stereotypical thinking." When we make decisions based off what we read, information may be false or taken out of context.

Low Maintenance vs. High Maintenance

When you think for yourself, you tend to be a lower maintenance individual rather than high maintenance. High maintenance students are those who believe that quantity of time in front of a teacher or professor is more important than the quality of the time. Such students were believed to be "sucking up" to a teacher or professor. Most educators admire students who are articulate and remain focused on the conversation at hand instead of meandering.

A low maintenance individual is one who follows the advice on a sign I once read on a business leader's desk. This sign read, "Lead, follow, do something, or else get the heck out of the way." Low maintenance students tend to figure things out quicker than higher maintenance students. The latter need more hand holding and specific directions. Students and colleagues who rely heavily on guidance will eventually fall behind since they lack the ability to problem solve themselves.

A trait of the low maintenance leader is one who lives by the following principle. That is, "While we necessarily have to have rules, policies, and laws—and we want our people to follow them—we also want our people to think."

Followers vs. Leaders

I was directly involved in a good story about a company policy that encouraged rules following. I purchased an umbrella in Boston, believing that it was spring loaded rather than a manual push-up. After I bought my umbrella, I walked out to the street where it was raining and opened it. Well, I discovered it was manual and not spring loaded. So, I returned to the same cashier at the same register where I had purchased my umbrella five minutes earlier. I explained my plight to her. Though she apologized, she pointed out the sign to the right of the cash register that said "All Sales Final."

I thought to myself, this is not going well. I had run into a follower and not a leader. (I differentiate between leadership and followership by saying that a follower actually does things right, but a leader does the right thing.)

I asked for the supervisor. When the supervisor arrived, she quickly refunded my money and apologized for my delay. Wait! Before you begin to jump on the bandwagon and feel sorry for the poor cashier because she did not have the authority to do anything, consider this. Didn't she have the authority to recognize that this was not what the store's particular policy was intended to prevent? She could have taken the initiative to contact her supervisor and explain the situation becoming a leader and not a follower. The cashier didn't think for herself.

Thinking for Yourself

You need to set your own goals, dreams, and desires, and not just accept those of others, including your parents. NO ONE really, really knows 100 percent what makes you happiest, and sometimes you don't even know. At least this is my premise. Students who are really happy at what they do tend to be more successful because they pursue their goals and dreams with a passion. Happiness and passion will more often trump grades any day in terms of life success. Show me someone who is passionate and happy about his own pursuit and I will bet that person will end up successful—at least in his or her own mind.

Coach's Corner

Several years ago, I had student majoring in marketing who claimed that nothing motivated him. He just enjoyed hanging out with his friends and playing poker when a game was available. He asked me what I thought about his poker playing since his parents were not keen on it. I sided with his parents. However, I did throw in the caveat that perhaps it could be a hobby he could pursue when he had a job because he was so passionate about it.

Three years later, he visited me outside the classroom. He explained that recently he won several thousand dollars playing poker as a hobby. To this day, I still am uncertain whether poker is just a hobby or a career with him. Nevertheless, my guess is that he is happy either way— or at least I hope so!

My own father wanted me to be a newspaperman just like him. My mother even worked for the newspaper. I liked journalism. I loved my parents. However, I was not exactly passionate about journalism, and it did not make me completely happy. Sure, journalism can make others happy and create a worthwhile career for them. However, the more passionate and happier fit for me came through helping develop salespeople, sales managers, and coaching college students.

There is an old saying:

> He who knows and knows not that he knows
> he is asleep so awaken him.
> He who knows not and knows that he knows
> not is a child so teach him.
> He who knows not and knows not that he
> knows not is a fool so avoid him.
> He who knows and knows that he knows is a
> wise man so follow him.

Students who know and know that they know tend to make the best original thinkers and do not follow the crowd. How does one even begin to rise to this level of knowing?

Well, it's actually pretty simple. You should begin by recognizing that when you hear one side of a story that there are always two sides.

Let's move to the *Coach's Playbook* to identify key points for improving this particular lesson of leadership.

COACH'S PLAYBOOK

Think for Yourself—Don't Just Follow

1. One leader used to say that when he heard two sides of a story, the answer usually lay somewhere in between. Don't become attached to only one idea or one way. Think of the flipside.

2. The majority CAN BE right, but the majority CAN BE WRONG. This realization will challenge you to discern when the majority is RIGHT and when they are WRONG. It is not always easy, but it is easier to think for yourself and not be influenced by others when you have had time to think through it on your own.

3. I recall the movie *Dead Poet's Society,* starring Robin Williams as a teacher at an elite eastern prep school. The movie's message was simple: Do you want to group think or do you want to think as an individual? Unfortunately, Robin Williams's character was fired since he did not follow the group think mentality .Although the headmaster did not like him, his students loved the freedom to think on their own.

4. Finally, recognize that any leader or low maintenance person may not always make the right decision, but they do have the power to make the decision right! Be willing to acknowledge your errors when you make them, because everyone makes mistakes in life. It is unavoidable!

LAUGH IT OFF –
DON'T TAKE YOURSELF TOO SERIOUSLY
(Nobody Else Does!)

*"With the fearful strain that is on me night and
day, if I did not laugh I should die."*
—Abraham Lincoln

. . . .

Most students in high school and college enjoy laughing, but find it difficult to laugh at themselves. The reasons are simple. They take themselves too seriously. They fear being viewed as unintelligent. They do not want to be seen as being failures. They fear being the type of person who deserves to be made fun of. Such students, consciously or subconsciously, feel that the world revolves around them and their high aspirations—why shouldn't they be taken seriously?

Learn to Laugh at Yourself

Unfortunately, if such students asked their friends, they might be surprised to learn that their friends believe the world revolves around them. When you view life from this perspective, it is a struggle to laugh at yourself when things aren't going well or when people are poking fun at you. But why miss out on the fun? Certainly, if others can do things to make you laugh, at some point, you're sure to have something to offer as well!

Laughter Makes You Human

It's okay to be a serious-minded individual, but that doesn't have to prevent you from being self-deprecating. President John F. Kennedy elevated this skill to an art form during his time in office. Once, it was suggested that his father, a well-to-do businessman named Joseph P. Kennedy, had a hand in buying votes in Illinois during the 1960 presidential election to help his son secure the office. In response, the president read a telegram from his father. The telegram said, "Don't buy a single more vote than is necessary. I'll help you win this election, but I'll be damned if I'm going to pay for a landslide!"

Laughter Makes You Relatable

After he was elected, Kennedy also deflected criticism that his brother Robert was not qualified to be the attorney general of the United States.

Kennedy reportedly remarked, "I don't see anything wrong with giving Bobby a little legal experience before he goes out on his own to practice law." Later during his presidency, Kennedy was asked about the fairness of the media's coverage of his administration. He replied, "Well, I'm reading more and enjoying it less."

Kennedy was able to laugh himself, and his wit has been well remembered. To some people, it made him more human and relatable. One theory suggests that people tend to trust those who can laugh at themselves, primarily because they possess the self-confidence to weather good-natured teasing and even more serious criticism. Such people know how to stay grounded.

Coach's Corner

On the first day of each semester, I explain to new students that if they believe they can stay anonymous in my class, they should rethink taking it. No one is immune to my digs because it's important that the students learn it is okay to perform poorly or fail altogether.

During the first part of the class, I grade the students on their articulation skills. Most grades are either a D or an F. Students at the Kelley School of Business are horrified that they could receive a failing score, even though it doesn't count toward any semester or exam grades. After a few weeks, they start to realize that failure is acceptable as long as they can identify areas in which to make progress. One student, sounding a little like Kennedy, asked me, "Professor, do you think I have a chance of becoming a D student?" The class laughed with her.

In context, her question is even funnier. The Kelley School of Business's admission process is no joke. Students need to be in the top 10 percent of their high school class and have impressive scores on their ACT or SAT tests. This particular student had a 3.7 GPA, but she accepted that she struggled with her articulation skills, took it in stride, and set a goal for improvement.

It's All About Perspective

Several years ago, I posed a relatively simple question regarding whether a particular type of sale was considered transactional or consultative. The student began by saying, "Well, it all depends on whether the customer believes it is a high-risk decision to them or not. If the customer perceives it as a high-risk decision, it would be classified as a consultative sale. If not, it would be considered a transactional sale."

Not a bad answer, but he didn't stop there. He explained the characteristics of each type of sale and gave an example and another and another. His completely accurate 30-second response stretched out for five unnecessary minutes.

Naturally, he became fodder for one of my zingers. I replied, "Are you sure you want to be a marketing major? It sounds like you would be better suited for politics."

To his credit, he got in on the joke and I complimented him for laughing at himself. It was the most important lesson he could take away from the experience. It turned out he was a likable and self-effacing person. He was able to put life in the proper perspective. He recognized that in any situation, we can choose to laugh or choose to cry and sulk.

He recently received his first promotion to assistant brand manager, a coveted position with a blue-chip company. It wouldn't surprise me to learn that a contributing factor in his career rise was his ability to play well with others and not take himself too seriously.

So if one of the key reasons this student and others understand that life involves learning to laugh at yourself and stop taking things too personally, how exactly do you do it? I would recommend the following three steps, informed by psychology.

Let's move to the *Coach's Playbook* to identify key points for improving this particular lesson of laughing at yourself.

COACH'S PLAYBOOK

*Laugh It Off—**Don't** Take Yourself Too Seriously*

1. Recognize that you are only the most important person in the world to yourself. Be cognitive that people do not take you as seriously as you think.

2. Everyone else is the most important person in their own eyes, so why try to compete against them?

3. Recognize that life is actually funny. People are funny. Funny things happen. You do some pretty funny things, which would be a whole lot more funny if you just acknowledged them! If

---

doubt this hypothesis, ask yourself where comedians draw inspiration from for their greatest routines. The answer is from their observations about how people behave.

4. Just try it. Choose to laugh instead of feeling angry or frustrated when you fail. Everyone makes choices in life, and your decision to laugh it off might be the catalyst that helps turn your life around. Try it on five separate occasions and notice the difference in people's reactions around you. You'll endear yourself to others by making them more comfortable and keeping them entertained.

Life Lesson Eight

SEEK OUT INFORMATION –
DON'T ASSUME ANYTHING

"I think that probably the most important thing about our education was that it taught us to question even those things we thought we knew."
—Thabo Mbeki

When you reflect on the American education system, does it seem that we reward our students for answers and not questions? Wouldn't it be interesting if we inverted the grading system and rewarded students for asking intriguing questions rather than having all the answers? Sometimes I wonder if our education system destroys creativity with this emphasis on knowing everything.

Why in the world would we want to do that? Isn't our education system about gaining knowledge in such disciplines as calculus, literature, biology, finance, marketing, history, and physics? That is the ultimate goal, but should it be?

An Open Perspective Promotes Creativity

Through my career and in the classroom, I have found that the best students, professors, and managers are constantly asking questions. What kind of leaders would they be if they assumed they knew everything? What kind of impression does it give their peers if they do not embrace open-ended conversation, opinions, or other ways of doing things? Crunching facts without seeking meaning behind the answers ultimately holds us back.

Research Says

Consider Ronald Vale's *Molecular Biology of the Cell* article, "The Value of Asking Questions," In the piece, he encourages active questioning instead of "fact finding." When students become too focused on the facts and the end result, they sacrifice the exploratory process necessary to actually solve a problem. Memorization without proper reasoning only goes so far. Assumptions are made, and ideas are shut off and ignored. Narrow-minded vision becomes the norm.

While Vale touches on the root of scientific processes, the article centers on our education system and how the classroom structure has skewed how we perceive questions. Some view it as a point of weakness instead of an opportunity to learn. What is the source of this idea? Vale presents the following "cultural factors" that create barriers, both for students in the classroom and people in their careers:

First is the perception that the teacher is an almighty vessel of knowledge who imparts information to students.... However, that view is unfair to teachers. Teachers also need to be students. A teacher should feel completely comfortable saying, "I do not know the answer to that question, but let me look it up—or let's look it up together."

A second impediment to using questioning as an educational tool is that questions are unpredictable by their nature... The ability to ask a question, research the answer, and present it to the class requires some degree of flexibility.

Never skip to the facts. Did Christopher Columbus adhere to the notion that the world was flat? While the truth is clear to us today, someone had to question the assumption to actually disprove it. Questions like why is the Earth's shadow round during a solar eclipse opened the door to a world of possibilities.

Active probing should be the premises for seeking answers. When professors and managers encourage open-ended questions, they invite different perspectives, adopt new approaches, and solve wider problems. While some may make assumptions, it is always better to clarify. A question unasked today is a mistake to be known tomorrow.

Questions: Quality Over Quantity

When you move from the classroom to a career, the questions you ask—or don't ask—will shape your path in the workplace. No matter how underrated it may be, the practice of asking good questions is the most empowering skill set we can acquire. Those *good* questions hold the key to your success. The smarter the question you ask, the better the answer will be.

Coach's Corner

During the 1970s, Xerox dominated the world of copiers, but the company was beginning to lose market share. At the time, I worked as a national account manager and sales manager for the company. We invested considerable time persuading customers that our equipment worked as well, if not better, than products from the competition. Xerox's corporate leaders posed an important question: How can we provide more feature-rich equipment with excellent copy quality?

Enter Japanese manufacturers. They examined the U.S. marketplace and asked: How can we manufacture our equipment to work better than the Xerox equipment? How can we generate more copies between service calls?

If they had been asked, the field sales force would have told Xerox senior management that customers were not happy with the reliability of our products regardless of what the service printouts showed. Buyers believed that Japanese-manufactured machines were more reliable—and they were.

Of course, the story doesn't end there. Japanese manufacturers were able to sell their copiers for what it cost Xerox to manufacture their machines. Customers said that the Japanese-made copiers cost less and ran better. Fortunately, Xerox was able to turn the tables in the mid-1980s.

This story explains why questions are so important. Asking the wrong question can lead to poor choices in the business world, politics, education, and athletics. The senior officials at Xerox had asked themselves a question, but it didn't address their customers' needs. This decision cost them revenue and profit that went to their competitors.

Something similar occurred in the automotive industry during the 1970s and 1980s. American automobile manufacturers began to think in terms of shortening the time from the drawing board to the assembly line to provide the latest auto features for their buyers. However, *Consumer Report*'s automobile reliability ratings greatly favored Japanese-made vehicles over American-made cars. Toyota and Honda made their imprint on American soil. Though the American public wanted to remain loyal, they preferred to purchase cars that had fewer mechanical problems.

Again, Toyota and Honda were focused on reliability and asked themselves: How well does this auto run? Is it dependable? How can we make reliable automobiles?" The questions that American manufacturers asked were secondary in the mind of Japanese manufacturers. Such questions were asked only after they addressed the issue of dependability. That is, the companies that succeeded in both the Xerox example and the car example asked not only smart questions but did so after seeking out information rather than giving it. The companies that lost market share asked the wrong questions because they were giving answers rather than seeking them. Remember what I said about the importance of listening?

Eventually, Six Sigma and other Leadership Thru Quality programs were developed in America to address reliability issues. American business leaders finally realized that the way to catch up to Japanese companies was to focus on reliability, something Japanese companies had been doing since the 1970s.

It's not only important to seek information. It's important to seek the right information. An effective way to do that is by working through the three solutions I've provided, all of which focus heavily upon practice, practice, and more practice.

Let's move to the *Coach's Playbook* to identify key points for improving this particular lesson of seeking.

COACH'S PLAYBOOK

*Seek out **Information**—Don't Assume Anything*

1. Practice asking questions into a recording device such as your smartphone. Ask as many questions as quickly as you can for one minute regarding a particular topic. You've been conditioned during upwards of 18 years of schooling to provide answers, so learning to seek information instead of giving it may require a shift in your behavior.

2. Focus on asking smart questions rather than just any type of question. Smart questions are ones that others may not have thought about and that provoke new ideas on a topic. The person who controls the questions controls the conversation.

3. Train yourself not to feel compelled to disclose unsolicited information unless it really pertains to the conversation at hand. Stay focused. Remember that questions display concern and care for others.

MAXIMIZE TIME OR NEVER FIND IT

"Don't wait. The time will never be just right."
—Napoleon Hill

. . . .

Many students (and adults) feel as if their lives are spinning out of control at times. We have all dealt with juggling too much, saying yes, or committing to too many obligations. However, we don't always realize how detrimental this can be on our quality of life.

When people feel that they are losing control, they push it aside, pretend it's normal, or try to ignore its consequences. Yet, there is no denying reality. When our lives get out of control, we begin to lose control.

Distractions Are Detrimental

With so much to juggle, is it any wonder that people are cramming more and more into their work or school day with the same outcome? There doesn't seem to be enough time in the day to get it all finished.

Because of today's technology, we are members of a society accustomed to almost instantaneous responses to smartphone queries via texts, emails, and phone calls. While smartphones are a tool for communicating and enable us to become more efficient, they often have the opposite effect.

Don't confuse this argument as contradicting lesson four. Yes, it is important to be prompt, on time, and responsive. However, do you need to dedicate your time and energy to *everybody* and *everything* all at once? This is where people fall short. They have a misconception that all things must be addressed immediately, no matter how insignificant something may be. They ultimately lose sight of the end goal.

Accomplishing Goals

Nearly everyone has set goals at some point, perhaps related to athletics, academics, careers, or the personal such as weight loss. Sometimes people achieve these goals, and sometimes they do not. This raises a question. Why do some students achieve their goals, while others do not?

I believe the answer is simpler than people like to think.

Many people, adults and students alike, find it very difficult to manage their time. Numerous requests pop up throughout the day. Those who can prioritize what needs to be accomplished when—and act upon it—are the ones who ultimately end up reaching their goals. They can differentiate between tasks that are crucial to complete and those that are less important to complete.

Those who fall short of their goals become too overwhelmed by the surplus of tasks and lose sight of priorities. Instead of maximizing time, they simply lose time. Once they lose their time, they never find it.

How Do You Spend Your Time?

There are only 168 hours in each week. If we sleep eight hours per day, we spend 56 hours sleeping per week. This leaves us with 112 hours per week, or 16 hours per day, to accomplish everything that needs to be done.

Research Says

Therese Hoff Macan explains the significance of our perception of control in an article in the *Journal of Applied Psychology*, "Time Management: Test of a Process Model." The author supports the idea that time management has always been linked to better results, whether it's in a workplace, organization, or household. Macan proposes that it's our perception of time that really matters. It is only when we change our perception that these better outcomes emerge. Otherwise, we would not be able to achieve the balanced frame of mind for which we all strive.

Just as we get rid of stress by reducing the level of stress indicators or changing the way we perceive them, Macan argues that we can gradually gain more of our time by changing our frame of mind. She wrote:

> Those who perceive that they have control over their time should experience fewer frustrations and tensions in response to their job (job-induced tension) than those who do not perceive themselves as having such control. Furthermore, those who perceive themselves to have control over time should report fewer physiological symptoms of stress (somatic tension). In effect, those who perceive themselves to have control over time should be healthier employees.

Of course, our perception of control will not change without taking action or making a conscious effort to improve our behaviors, Those who adopt the right behaviors and learn how to manage their allotted time ultimately gain a perception of control, a perception that thematically matches what we've discussed in other lessons regarding taking responsibility for oneself, particularly when it comes to one's actions and behaviors.

There is no shortage of books on the subject of time management, but does it really take a book to change your life? If an individual were to follow the four simple steps outlined in the *Coach's Playbook*, they would be more likely to take control of their time and life.

Preparation vs. Procrastination

Coach's Corner

Occasionally at the end of a semester, there are students who come to me explaining that they have three or four exams within a given week. They ask if they can take my exam a couple days later. It is difficult for me to accommodate such requests because I think the central problem is that students don't know how to effectively manage their time to take three exams in one week.

Am I being too harsh regarding the students? For the most part, I don't think so. Many students typically begin earnestly studying for an exam two days before it is taken. So, if an exam is scheduled for a Wednesday, they begin studying on Monday. Why wouldn't they just prepare to study a week in advance if they know when each exam is scheduled? Would the same concept be applied in the workforce once they graduate? I like to take a realistic approach when teaching my students. In this case, I try to enforce practices and habits that prepare them for the real world.

There are a percentage of students who keep up with their school work. They read the assignments in the textbook, review their class notes, and perform the exercises suggested. These students are much less likely to feel overwhelmed when they are confronted with three exams in one week.

Unfortunately, as previously mentioned, this pattern doesn't change much when people move into their careers. They feel like they lose control of their time and life, particularly when they move into management. In management, there are so many targets, objectives, and balls to juggle that it can feel very overwhelming.

For example, a manager's boss may require a report by the end of the week, two of the manager's direct reports need help with their projects, the family needs to visit Aunt Emma, and there are two boards on the porch that need replacement. It is so easy to feel like your life is spiraling out of control and there is not enough time to get it all done.

Just remember that once you lose time, you can never find it! How do you not lose it? Let's explore four steps we might take. Let's move to the *Coach's Playbook* to identify key points for improving this particular lesson on time management.

COACH'S PLAYBOOK

Maximize Time or Never Find It

1. Each morning, list the activities that need to be accomplished during the day. For students, the list may include the following:

   Meet with professor (30 minutes), fraternity or sorority meeting (1.5 hours), study time (4 hours), call your boyfriend or girlfriend (30 minutes), attend intramural basketball practice (1 hour), meet BFF at Student Union for coffee, repair flat tire, buy new phone, etc.

2. Prioritize each of these activities as A, B, or C. Then, prioritize them further: A1, A2, A3, B1, B2, B3, B4, C1, C2, C3, and C4.

   A's must get done, or else there are significant repercussions. For example, if you don't study, you may not pass an exam. Or if you don't go to a major event on campus, your relationship with that person or organization may be jeopardized.

   B's are important and will need to be tackled, but you would survive if they aren't accomplished today. For example, you might be able to borrow toothpaste if you were out of it, so going to buy more would be a B for the day and not an A.

   C's are those items that would be nice to do, but if they didn't get done there wouldn't be any repercussions. For example, stopping by food court with a friend to grab an hour lunch and socialize when there simply is not enough time in a day to do the A's and B's. Reschedule the lunch to a more convenient time for the both of you later in the week.

It may sound easy, but ask yourself a question. Do you do the B's and C's before the A's, because the A's are either overwhelming or uncomfortable?

A job search might be overwhelming and uncomfortable for you. In the classroom or student life, it might be having that tough discussion with a professor because you have had an incredible amount of personal issues that particular semester and you need to figure out a solution, but you perceive the professor to be too strict to help you. What should be your game plan with such an uncomfortable A?

3. The delay in addressing A's brings us to the third step. How do you bring yourself to address the A's that are overwhelming or uncomfortable—or both? If they are overwhelming, break the item down into smaller parts. Only do a bit of that item each day.

For example, the 20-page paper may be broken down like this:

- On day one, you gather the research material together you will need.
- On day two, you review the material.
- On day three, you put together an outline.
- On day four, you begin writing, but you only do 10 percent of the paper.
- On day five, you write another 10 or 15 percent.
- And so on...

The point is that you don't wait until the last minute to begin a 20-page project. If it is due in a month, you begin the project the next day. It is okay if your project is completed 10 days before the due date. In doing so, you are able maintain control of your time and life.

I fully recognize that being that early on a project is almost unheard of. However, as a personal aside, I have completed many such projects on this schedule when I write training modules. I apply this guideline to each and every one of them for fear of not meeting a deadline with the best work I could do. The extra 10 days gives me time to review and edit the project so it is my best work. Naturally, someone else may not think it is a best work, but you and I can only do the best we can do, right?

Now what if the A is uncomfortable? Let's discuss the aforementioned personal issues during a particular semester and the delay discussing the issue with a perceived strict professor. Of course, it is uncomfortable for you. It would be uncomfortable for the majority of us. However, the more you delay in addressing the situation, the worse it gets. I know this from first-hand experience during my undergraduate days. So what do you do? You list the consequences that will affect you if you don't address this uncomfortable situation on a piece of paper. This list might look something like this:

- You received a lower grade. In college you might be able to take a grade of Incomplete. Then, the professor provides you an extended period of time to complete your assignments.
- You feel bad about yourself.
- You lose respect in eyes of teacher/professor or peers or parents.

- You recognize that you are unable to confront and resolve conflict which is very difficult to avoid in life.
- It becomes more difficult to gain admittance to further education.
- You embarrass yourself to yourself, possible reducing your self-esteem. You know you should do something but you procrastinate and that usually does not create a good feeling inside.

4. Finally, you can always delegate portions of some projects. We are absolutely NOT suggesting you have anyone do any writing for you. However, you are permitted to use various research resources to identify articles, quotes, or ideas that might help you with the project. This approach works particular well with group projects in which each team member is assigned a particular part of the project to work on. For example, one student will write the introduction to the project, another will be responsible for the PowerPoint presentation, and still yet another will be accountable for writing the remaining part of the paper after the introduction.

In the professional world, many parts of a project can be delegated. Your employer would most likely recommend it. Managers do this routinely in the real world.

There is one note of caution. Delegation is not as easy as it sounds. While delegation is good, you never want to delegate a task to someone that believes you are delegating it to them because you just don't want to do it yourself. This results in the perception that you are above doing work. This is not a good perception to foster. Explain to the person why you are delegating this project.

It would be nice if you could explain why the team will benefit from it. For instance, your strengths are in creative PowerPoint presentations. It would be a big help to the group if you could make the team stand out in front of the audience.

When you lose time, you never find it again. However, if you apply these techniques to your everyday life, you won't have to worry about losing it in the first place.

THINK OF OTHERS – DON'T BE SELF-ORIENTED

"No one is useless in this world who lightens the burdens of another."
—Charles Dickens

. . . .

At the beginning of each semester, I ask my students who they believe is the most important living person in the world. I give them three minutes to ponder the question. Their answers have included the president of the United States, the Pope, LeBron James, and Hillary Clinton. Their parents, their grandparents, and Jesus also get mentioned.

Rarely do they get the correct answer—themselves. I explain that each person has a tattoo on their chest that says, I Like Me. After more than 30 years of college teaching, no student has disagreed with me, even though they are encouraged to share opposing viewpoints from day one.

Me, Myself, and I

Yes, you think life is all about you. To an extent, it is. But life is also about others. Motivational speaker Zig Zigler captured that idea when he said, "You can have everything in life you want, if you will just help enough other people get what they want."

Chalk it up to karma, but helping others also indirectly links to the pinnacle of psychologist Abraham Maslow's hierarchy of needs. In this hierarchy, he introduces the concept of self-actualization. According to Maslow, the final level in his pyramid of needs is reached when a person begins to exhibit creativity and seek self-fulfillment. Just like Zigler, he maintains that fulfillment can be reached by helping others achieve what you have achieved. How can you do this when your focus is only on you?

If we accept the premise that the person you are talking to is the most important person in the world because they would recognize in their heart that they were if asked, then why don't we treat each other better? It is because we don't care about others and care too much about ourselves? I don't think so. It's more likely that we forget the world doesn't revolve around us, but that it revolves around everybody.

Is there anything wrong with believing you are the most important person in the world? No, because it's accurate. What is wrong is when we get so tied up in ourselves that others constantly become second or third on our list of priorities. It's certainly okay to grant other people the title of "Most Important Person in the World" for a while and focus on helping them without expecting any payment in return. Today's mind frame, however, seems to be all about me.

Research Says

In "Is Today's Society Too Self-Centered?" published on the New Times website, Sandra Diamond Fox describes research conducted by psychology professor Jean Twenge. Narcissism—defined as "the excessive interest in one's own importance, abilities, appearance, and comfort" in the article—is more prevalent now than it ever used to be, according to Twenge. The professor added, they also "tend to be more aggressive and less likely to help others."

Fox also highlighted some key figures. In a work value study on a nationally representative sample of U.S. high school seniors in 1976,

1991, and 2006, Twenge found leisure values increased steadily over the generations.

Extrinsic values, such as status and money, were also rated higher among the current generation of young people than they were among baby boomers. Social values, such as making friends, and intrinsic values, such as having an interesting, results-oriented job, were rated lower by generation me than by baby boomers.

On a positive note, those who do remember to take the "Me" badge off sometimes undoubtedly reap benefits far greater than those who focus solely on themselves. People notice when you take a step back and place your attention on others, and it does make a difference.

One of my former students put it this way: "When I know that someone has my back and is looking out for me, I am more likely to want to help that person because they care about me. I want to be on their team." It is indeed easier to want to help others when you feel others want to help you and will put you first at times.

It's so easy for students to forget that parents, business leaders, athletes, music icons, actors, and teachers are people too. It doesn't occur to a student that if they don't attend a lecture and instead visit with me to learn what they missed, I am, in effect, teaching the class twice. Instead, I break students into teams of four or five each semester and encourage them to catch up with each other to fill in the blanks.

Coach's Corner

Jeff Wuslich—one of my former students and a co-founder of the Global Sales Leadership Society (GSLS; now the Global Sales Workshop)—was a leader on the Indiana University campus. After graduation, he eventually became chief of staff to the university's chancellor. Currently, Jeff owns a distillery in Bloomington and is a major fundraiser for a U.S. Senate candidate.

I was honored to receive an invitation to attend his wedding. During the ceremony, one of his groomsmen made a comment that everyone thought the groom was their best friend. Jeff had a knack for making others feel like they were the most important people in the world.

In one of my first encounters with Jeff, we had scheduled a meeting in my office to discuss recruitment and the fledgling GSLS. Due to my hectic schedule, the meeting had to be held over the lunch hour. Jeff offered to bring the food. At our appointed time, he arrived with a hot plate of spaghetti and meatballs, a vegetable dish, and a Diet Cherry Coke, which he knew I liked. He handed me a cloth napkin and actual knives and forks—not the plastic kind.

We had an extremely productive lunch meeting. Don't be skeptical or cynical regarding his motives. Nearly everyone who knows Jeff would say that's just the way he is and that he focuses on others much more than he focuses on himself. It is in his nature. My point is that there are people who are willing to forget about themselves and invest in the message of this lesson. Don't be self-oriented—it's about others!

As former U.S. politician and education reformer Horace Mann would assert, "Doing nothing for others is the undoing of ourselves." I'm not suggesting that you quit being selfish. I am proposing you recognize that selfishness is a matter of degrees. The more frequently you can put others before yourself, the more likely you are to be happy and successful.

Lou Holtz, the legendary Notre Dame football coach, told his players that everyone asks themselves three universal questions when interacting with another person:

1. Are you committed to excellence?
2. Can I trust you?
3. Do you care about me?

Most people want others to care about them. So, how do we learn to focus on others first?

In my experience, there are two approaches to helping others:

- When you both benefit or you simply benefit from helping another
- When there is absolutely no payoff to you for helping another except it makes you feel good

Dr. Ed Mitchell, a psychotherapist and personal friend, put it this way: "When we help someone unselfishly, we are still being somewhat selfish because it makes us feel good."

A Helping Hand

When I was a high school senior, I had a personal experience regarding unselfishness. At a high school journalism institute held at Indiana University, I met a gentleman named Al Spiers. At the time, Al was the editorial director of the Nixon Newspaper chain and a columnist for the *Michigan City Post-Dispatch*. Al was quite a character with a terrific sense of humor.

During my two weeks at this conference, he helped me with editing stories by conserving words and using better descriptive words. However, it didn't end there. We continued to exchange letters and Christmas cards for several years. I fully realized that I couldn't really do anything for him. It was nearly a one-way street in terms of unselfishness because it was a continual learning process for me, but what did Mr. Spiers get out of it? I don't think anything more than what Dr. Mitchell stated earlier. I believe it made him feel good.

I still have all these letters decades later because his writing style is so evident in the letters. His letters are almost like his newspaper columns that he was kind enough to send me.

Selfishness exists in a matter of degrees and total self-orientation won't get you anywhere in life. The only way to get where you want to go is by focusing on a few key things:

- Information seeking
- Offering help without being asked
- Chalking it up to karma

Read more about these important ideas in the solution section, and you will soon learn what a gift it truly is to focus on others instead of yourself. Therefore, let's move to the *Coach's Playbook* to identify key points for improving this particular lesson regarding self-orientation.

COACH'S PLAYBOOK

Think of Others—Don't Be Self-Oriented

1. Get into the habit of seeking information from others rather than giving it. This requires you to be willing to learn about others before you tell them about yourself. This may include asking questions such as: Where you are you from? Why did you come to this university? What organizations are you involved with or interested in?

    Though simple, these questions focus the limelight on others and not yourself. If you don't care about others, well, this lesson is going to create a few stumbling blocks for you. Remember that the primary way of displaying interest and concern is to ask questions and seek information from others. People will argue with statements, but questions are persuasive.

2. Offer to help others without waiting for them to ask you. One of my close high school friends, who later became an attorney and judge, used to tell me, "You don't need friends when things are going well. You need them when things are not going well. A true friend will not only help you if you ask, but offer to help you when you don't ask." I think the judge's advice is as good today as it was then.

3. Finally, chalk it up to karma! It always amazes me that throughout my life, the people I've seen that focused on helping others had great things come their way. Why? I could take a psychological perspective and say that people want to help those who help and care for them. No doubt, this is true. But I also want to point to karma, a force in the universe that causes good things to happen to good people who do good deeds. Try it! Everyone benefits when good deeds are repaid.

INDEX

C

D

H

I

J

K

L

M

ACKNOWLEDGEMENTS

From Dick Canada

We wish to acknowledge the Indiana University faculty at the Kelley School of Business. Over the years, faculty members contributed to the life lessons included in this book because of their strong leadership and role modeling of many of these lessons, especially Frank Acito, H. Shanker Krishnan, and Ann Bastianelli. Special thanks to Charlie Ragland for his insights regarding formatting.

My student and co-author Monica Anne Melink, truly exemplifies the life lessons in this book. Monica contributed research to this book and provided significant insights from a millennial perspective.

Three people deserve thank "yous" for their work in the copy editing phase of this book. Chelsea Caltuna handled recommended flow and wording, while Christina Edgington offered content suggestions and proofreading. Finally is Leslie Martin of Pearl Productions who used so many red marks that I'm convinced there will be a shortage of red pens in the near future—but all her comments were improvements!

Over the past 25 years, many students at the Kelley School of Business have provided me with many observations noted in these life lessons. These students include: Jay Preston, Chris Haimbach, Jeff Wuslich, Zac Engle, Angel Rivera, Lori Bellino, Garret Iden, Angela Shaul Fruits, Cassie Rodriquez, Nick Manigeri, Tony Corsaro, Shawn Heffren, Morgan Carite, and Ian Bobbitt.

My Speedway High School friends—Jack Fidger, Larry Thomas, Don Kutch, Sonny Sanders, Phil Engle, Rich Schwimmer and Doc Knoll—had a major impact on these life lessons over the decades, particularly during my formative years. Two of my dear college friends—Jon King and Bill Marshall—have as well and always make life fun!

Special mention to my friend David Hollensbe, whose professional counsel and strong friendship are exemplary. Also thanks to Russ Valentine, the modern day equivalent of Marcus Welby, MD., who recently passed away. May he rest in peace.

My business friends over the years have certainly had an influence on me, including Mark Bruin, Eldridge Bravo, Drew Maher, Mitch Radar, Paul Callahan, Chip Helm, and Jim Engledow. My pals from Xerox and Procter & Gamble have also lived these lessons including, William (Bill) G. Mays (in memoriam), Reverend Gregory Graham (in memoriam), Ted Rubley, Steve Iden, Suzy Yancey DuBois, John Pitz, Bridget Briede Momcilovich, and Sue Matchett.

Thanks to my terrific family, including my wife Debbie; our kids Andria and Graham, Erin and Greg, Jenny and Vince, and, David and Tracey; and our grandchildren Lily, Jackson, Peyton, Ciara, Logan, Alex W., Alex O., Andrew, Chase, and Ellie. I hope my grandchildren can use and appreciate the lessons in this book as they get older. Thanks also to Joe and Bev Cegala, the patriarch and matriarch of our Italian clan, along with Mike and Candy, Joe and Julie, David and Nanette, and many nieces and nephews.

Finally, my wonderful parents Lawrence M. and Violet R. Canada—who always set their expectation level of me to a solid C average performance in school and in life—deserve recognition as well. Somehow, I was always able to achieve their standards. Dad and Mom I wouldn't have had it any other way. You knew I would always feel like I had succeeded because your expectations of me were simply modest. You wanted me to be happy so you never pushed me to higher standards. You let me figure it out. You were the best!

ACKNOWLEDGEMENTS

From Monica Melink

First, I'd like to thank Steve and Mary Frances Melink. They were the best role models and parents I could ever ask for! Thank you for everything you have sacrificed for your four kids, for loving us (and each other) unconditionally, and for instilling the values that truly matter in life.

Thanks to Dad—the most passionate, hardworking, yet humble person I know—for inspiring me to chase my dreams. Thank you for being my hero and showing me the world's beauty.

Thanks to Mom—my constant, loving supporter, and channel of encouragement among everyday endeavors. Thank you for reminding me to smile, laugh, and to always be myself!

Thanks to my brother and sisters—Matt, Katie, and Laura—who consistently teach me patience, forgiveness, and other life attributes without even knowing it! You are my best friends through thick and thin. I admire each of you.

One life and professional coach to whom I cannot thank enough is Dick Canada, the author of this book and creator of *Top Ten Lessons*. To say you are a teacher is an understatement. You apply lessons that are essential in everyday life and focus on the principles that set people apart. It has been a privilege learning and working side by side with you. Indiana University and the Kelley School of Business have been changed for the better because of you.

Special thanks to my fiancé Dave Niehaus, for providing insight, encouragement, and for supporting me in whatever I do! You make me so happy, and never stop making me laugh.

Thanks to my Indiana University Women's Soccer family for being a source of inspiration behind these lessons, and for always stretching limits to achieve your goals. You have taught me that anything is possible.

Thanks to the Ursuline Academy's staff, faculty, and students for empowering women to make a difference and stand up for what we believe.

Thanks to Paul Callahan a "class-act leader" who never fails to put others before himself. Thank you for showing how to lead by example with resilience and passion, always showing appreciation to those around you.

I'd like to acknowledge the 2014 class of MDAs and other "Kraft Kids" for providing the gift of laughter, teamwork, and enthusiasm—and for never failing to make work fun.